ALFIE
THE
ALPHABET ANT

Learn To Read and Write

Back-To-Basics With Suze

Written & Illustrated
By
Joanne Suzette Ruiz

ALFIE
loves

____

Name

A a

Alfie eats an apple

a - a - a - a - apple

B b

Alfie rides a bike
b - b - b - b - bike

C c

Alfie carries a corn

c- c - c - c - corn

D d

Alfie plays with a dog

d - d - d - d - dog

D d D d D d D d D d D d

D d

E e

Alfie eats an egg

e - e - e - e - egg

F f

Alfie catches a fish

f - f - f - f - fish

G g

Alfie crawls in the grass
g - g - g - g - grass

G g G g G g G g G g G g

G g

H h

Alfie wears a hat
h - h - h - h - hat

H h Hh H h Hh H h Hh H h Hh H h Hh

Hh

I i

Alfie sees the ivy

i - i - i - i - ivy

JAM

J j

Alfie tastes the jam
j - j - j - j - jam

Jj Jj Jj Jj Jj Jj

Jj

Jj

K k

Alfie flies a kite
k - k - k - k - kite

L l

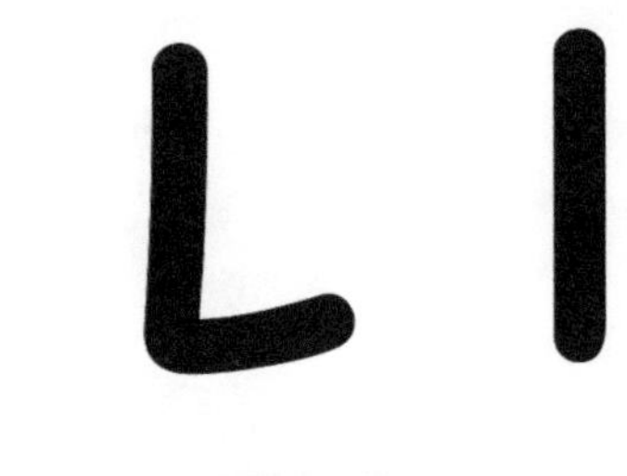

Alfie carries a leaf

l - l - l - l - leaf

M m

Alfie walks in the mud

m - m - m - m - mud

N n

Alfie sees the nest

n - n - n - n - nest

O o

Alfie sees the owl

o - o - o - o - owl

P p

Alfie sees the plane
p - p - p - p - plane

Q q

Alfie visits the queen

q - q - q - q - queen

R r

Alfie plays with a rabbit

r - r - r - r - rabbit

S s

Alfie enjoys the sun

s - s - s - s - sun

T t

Alfie climbs a tree

t - t - t - t - tree

U u

Alfie is under an umbrella

u - u - u - u - umbrella

V v

Alfie smells the violets

v - v - v - v - violets

W w

Alfie swims in the water

w - w - w - w - water

Xx

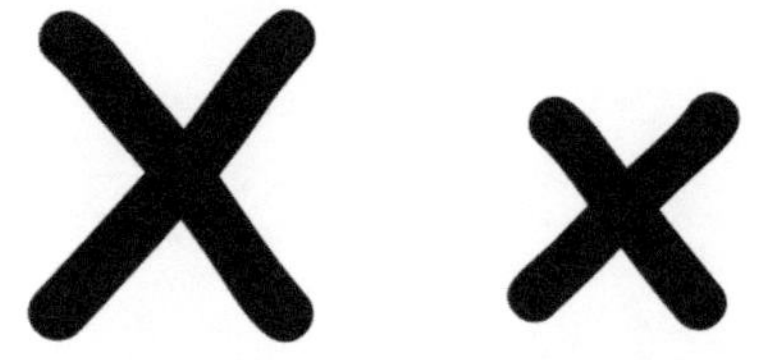

Alfie gets an xray

x - x - x - x - xray

Y y

Alfie eats yams

y - y - y - y - yams

ZOO

Z z

Alfie visits the zoo

z - z - z - z - zoo

Alfie the Alphabet Ant was created for parents with children 0 to 6 years old.
While using the wonderful gift of imagination, it is a fun way to focus
on the sound of each letter and reinforce that sound with writing practice.
This helps to build a strong foundation for speaking, reading and writing skills
in the early formative years so our precious children
are motivated to learn and eager to excel at school.
I hope you have as much fun reading this book with your little loved ones
as I had creating it!
Enjoy!

The End

ACHIEVEMENT

AWARDED TO

Date   Signature

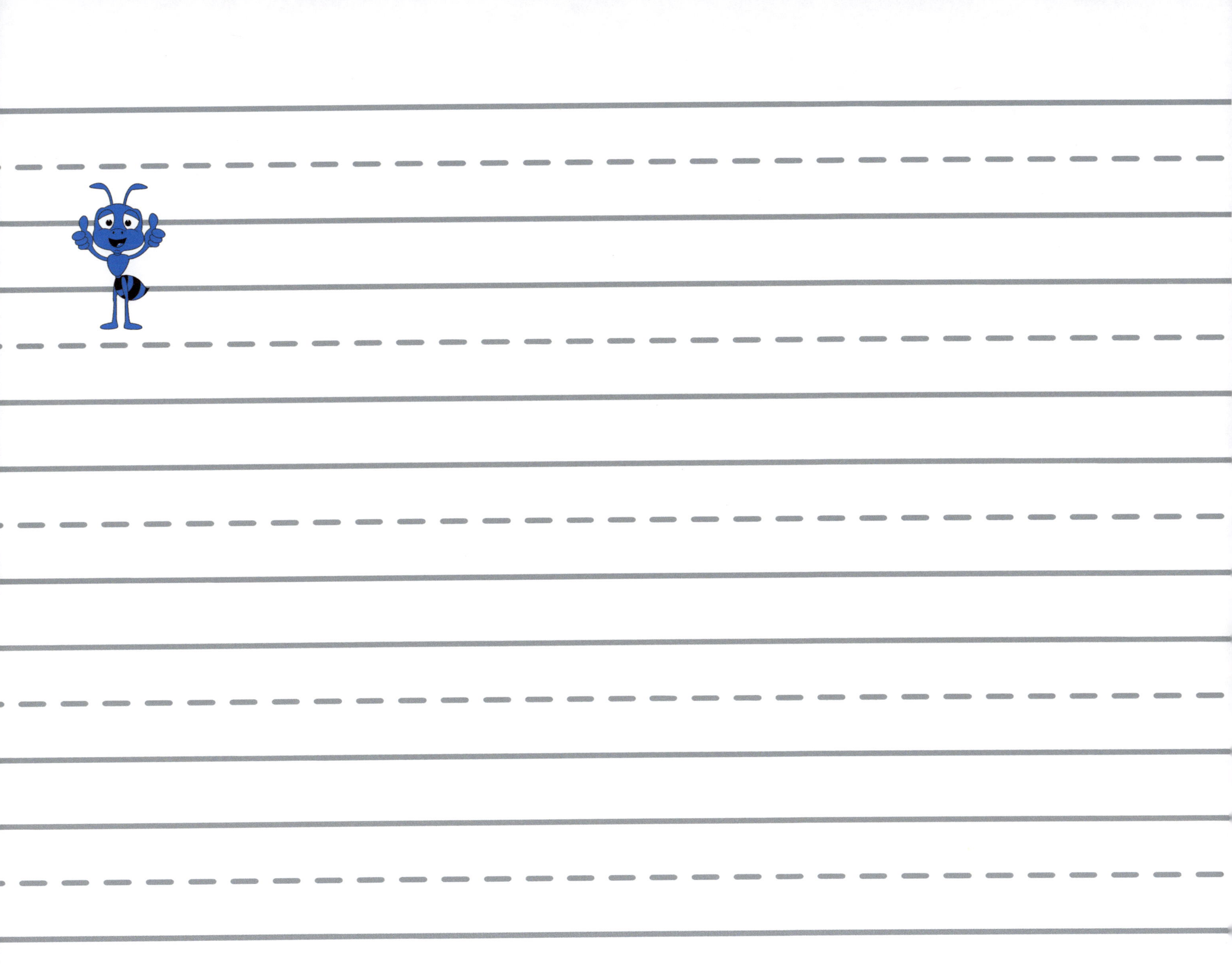

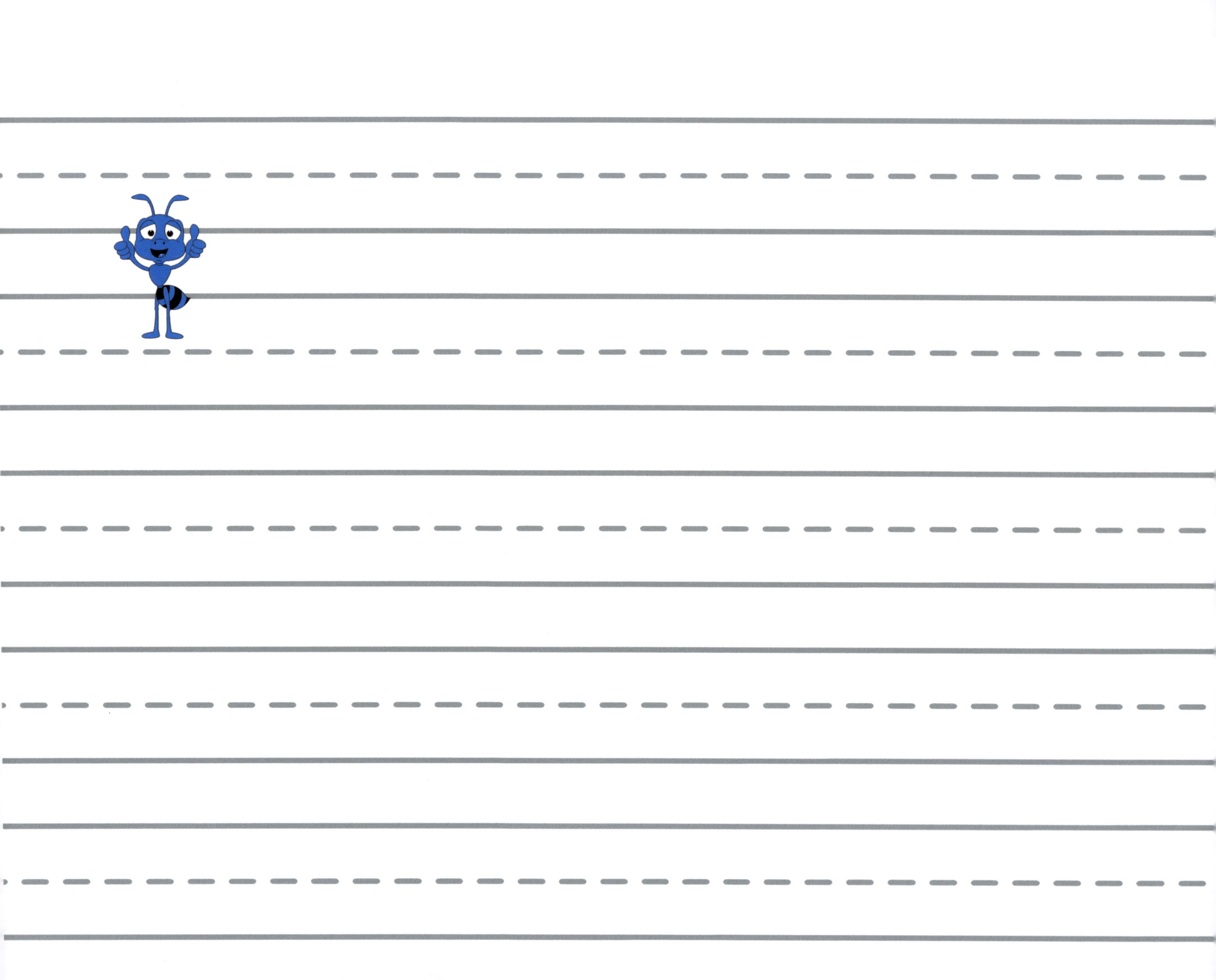

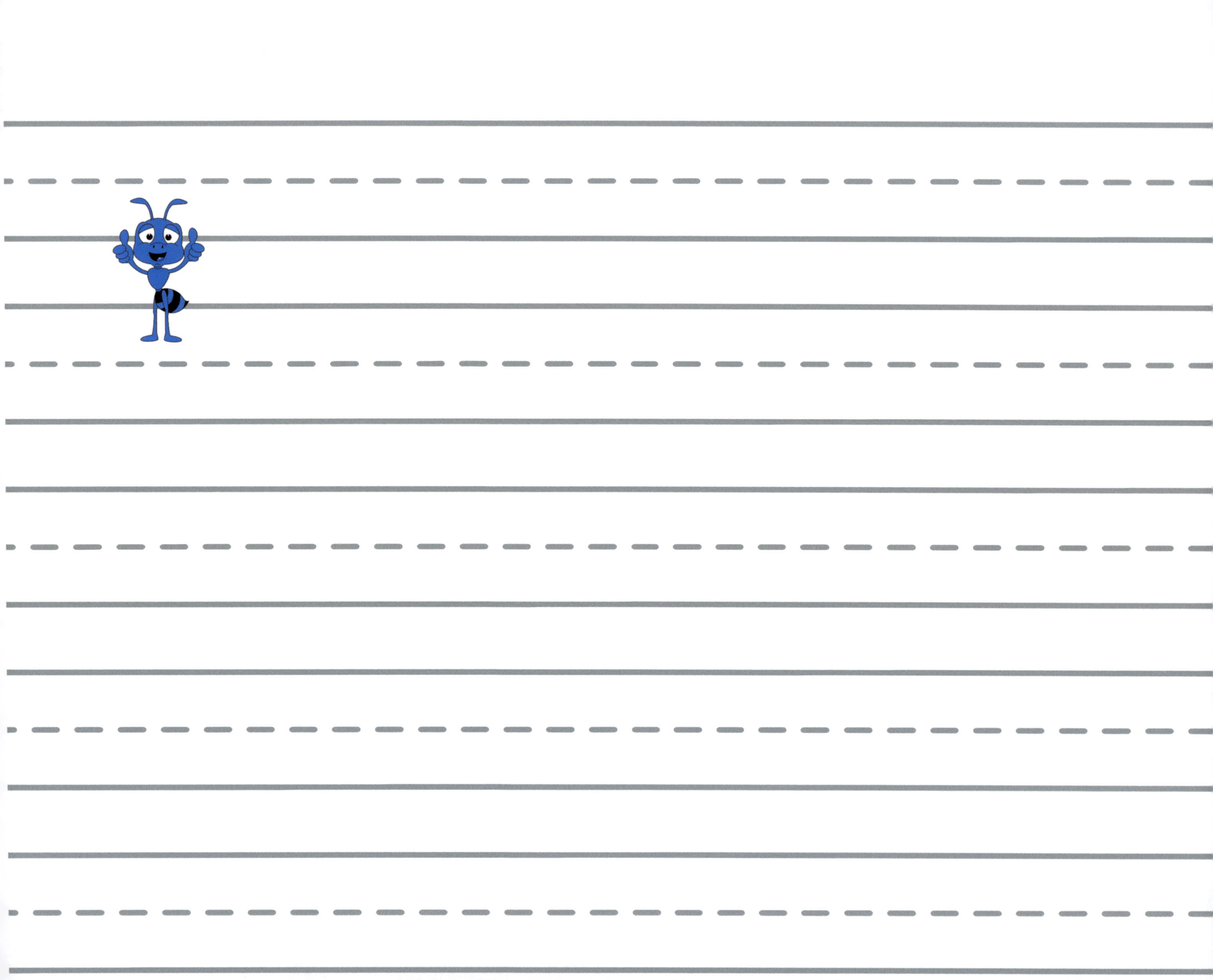